The Glory

of

Chief Washakie

Chief of the Shoshones

by
Ralph H. & Mary Tillman

Photogaraphs are reproduced courtesy of the Wyoming Division of Cultural Resources and the Pioneer Museum, Lander, WY.

Cover Photo: Wyoming Division of Cultural Resources

Paintings and drawings used in this book are by author Ralph Tillman and were photographed by Floyd Phillips, Shoshone tribal member.

For information contact: Filter Press, P.O. Box 95, Palmer Lake, CO 80133

ISBN 0-86541-043-7

Filter Press
Palmer Lake, Colorado
Printed in the United States of America

Dedication

This book is dedicated to the
Shoshone People

Painting by Ralph Tillman

Ralph H. Tillman
Great-great-grandson of
Chief Washakie

Foreword

Ralph H. Tillman, a great-great-grandson of Chief Washakie of the Shoshone Indians, was born on the Wind River Indian Reservation, Wyoming, in 1917.

At the early age of ten, Ralph showed an aptitude and talent for drawing, and could draw unusually fine horses. He had much opportunity to draw these animals, since he saw so many of them grazing upon the prairie around his home.

Ralph attended grade school at the Fort Washakie Government Indian School on the Reservation. After a short period spent at Lander, Wyoming, at the Lander High School, he entered Flandreau Vocational High School for Indians, in Flandreau, South Dakota. There he took the course in agriculture, as well as architecture and landscaping, and Indian arts and crafts. He was graduated after four years at Flandreau.

In 1942, at the beginning of World War II, he enlisted in the Army and served with the Corps of Engineers on the Aleutian Islands and on Okinawa. He was discharged December 27, 1945, and returned to his home at Wind River Indian Reservation. Because of his outstanding work while with the U.S. Army, he was recommended for

Officers' Training School but preferred to return home to help his family and be with his fellow tribesmen.

Once home, he took advantage of the GI Bill of Rights for World War II veterans and attended Montana State College at Bozeman, where he took college courses and a course in fine art. He studied oil and watercolor painting under well known art teacher, Otis Dozier. Later, he attended both the Indian Art School and Fine Arts School in Santa Fe, New Mexico, studying under the highly regarded art teacher, Alfred Morang. After this training Ralph's art work became known in Wyoming through numerous exhibitions and sales.

Other than the pursuit of his art, the most important thing in Ralph's life was his interest in the history and culture of the Shoshone people, his desire for their well-being, and pride in his heritage.

To honor Chief Washakie and the Shoshone Tribe Ralph and his wife, Mary, wrote this life story of the Chief from material gathered from historical sources and from information given to them by the Shoshone Indians themselves.

Mary (Mrs. Ralph H.) Tillman
Lander, Wyoming
March 1998

Chapter 1
An Auspicious Beginning

In a valley of the Bitteroot Range in Montana the teepees in the camp of the Flathead Indians looked like tall, white ghosts in the early morning light. The sun was tipping the rim of the mountains, its rays slowly dispelling the rolling, gray mist of the dawn. The year by white man's calendar was 1798.

From one of the teepees came the wail of a child. It was the first cry to the world of Chief Paseego's newly born son. Although outside the lodge all was quiet, the birth of the boy not yet known to the people, inside were gathered Paseego's family and the Head Chieftain of the Flathead tribe. The Chieftain held his arm outstretched over the little boy, about to put a strange-looking pendant around the tiny boy's neck. The pendant consisted of a flat, stone disk attached to a thong. On one side of the disk was drawn, crudely, a buffalo and on the other a mysterious sign that resembled a cross with the ends of its arms

1

turned backward, the symbol of the swastika, known and revered for its power in many lands and among many peoples, although this fact was unknown to most of the Indian people. The little boy's family watched with awe. Then, the eyes of his mother widened.

"I have seen that sign," she whispered. "I saw it once among my own people, the Shoshones to the south. Ah! It is great medicine!"

"Yes," said the Head Chief, sliding the pendant over the baby's head, "this is indeed of great medicine, and will always care for your son. For I say to you, this sign belongs with this child. He is the Chosen One of his people. My Sacred Power has told me so. This boy will grow to be a man who will lead this people to victory!"

The Chieftain left Paseego's lodge. Again the parents examined the talisman. What a wonderful thing had happened to them! Their son would be a leader of their people!

And indeed, the talisman was to guide Paseego's son throughout his life in his important quest for vision and strength.

When the boy was about five winters old,
tragedy struck his family. A Blackfeet war party
attacked and killed many in the Flathead camp.
Paseego was slain, and for days and weeks the boy,
his mother, and brothers and sisters wandered
homeless. One day the boy was separated from the
others and was struck down by a Blackfeet and left
for dead. He would have been scalped, but, as he
was such a small child, the warrior felt this would
bring him no honor. For some time, the boy lay
unconscious.

When he regained consciousness, he felt
weak. He felt a terrible pain in his head. He saw
that he lay close to a small stream, and, thirsty, he
drank of the water. The cool water lessened the
throbbing pain in his head.

Out of the sunset, a cloud of dust rolled
towards him, and emerging from it came four
horsemen. The boy thought they might be
strangers. One of them talked to him, but he could
not understand the language. Then he who was
the leader spoke in Flathead, saying they were
Shoshones. They asked why he was out there,

3

alone, on the plain. Where were his people? He replied that he was looking for his family and described the battle with the Blackfeet who had raided their camp. The Chief said that he and his three companions were from an Eastern group of Shoshones who were at this time hunting with a band of Lemhi Indians. They would take him to a place of safety, to their hunting camp.

The Shoshone leader reached down and swung the boy up behind him on his horse, and the party rode across the valley, soon arriving at a large camp. Suddenly, the young boy saw his mother and brothers running towards him. Joyously, he slid down from the horse and let his mother clasp him to her breast. She told him how she and her other children had roamed about until they had been found by these hunters.

He lived with his family among the happy, peace-loving band of Lemhis, through many winters. When his mother finally desired to return to the Flatheads and live again with them, her son stayed on with the Lemhis. They taught him everything he should know of hunting, tracking, sports, and all

other things a young man needed to learn. He
worthily defended the Lemhi people against their
enemies. As time went on, however, he discovered
that the warrior blood of his Flathead father spoke so
strongly within him, that he wished not only to
defend: he wished to go on warpaths and make a
name for himself. These Lemhis were too peaceful
to suit his bold spirit. Finally, he joined the ruthless
Bannock fighters. Soon, though, he found that even
the Bannock Indians were too heartless and cruel, in
their stealing and savagery to suit him. He could not
tolerate such meanness. He left the Bannocks and
made his way towards the people of his mother, the
Eastern Shoshones.

He took the mountain trails eastward to their
country, into what later became the state of
Wyoming. Following the course of the Green River,
he spotted herds of feeding antelope and buffalo in
this rich land. At last he saw the Shoshone camp by
the river and went to the lodge of their leader, Pah-
da-he-wa-kun-da, 'The Hiding Bear.' This old
patriarch was head of all Eastern Shoshones, and the
boy addressed him and explained that his mother

was a Shoshone and his father a Flathead, and he, himself, was eager to join the Shoshones under Pah-da-he-wa-kun-da and to cast his lot with them. The venerable Chief welcomed him into the tribe. He told him that he could prove himself the very next day when a buffalo hunt would be held.

The young man soon showed what a fine hunter he was, for he brought down a large buffalo bull with a single obsidian-tipped arrow. The women came to butcher the animal. He took his knife and cut an oval piece of hide which lay between the horns, rode back to camp with it, and fashioned a rattle out of this hide by stretching it over a gourd filled with pebbles. He had a fine tenor voice and a wonderful sense of rhythm, and often amused himself by singing all kinds of songs. Now he accompanied himself with his rattle, as the people gathering around him to listen agreed that he should be called Washakie— 'The Rattler.' From then on they spoke his new name.

"I like that," said the young man. "My name is Washakie," and he began another song:

My name is Washakie, the Rattler!
With my rattle, I sing my songs.
I sing for joy, because I am a good hunter
And have proved my worth to my people.

My name is Washakie, the Rattler!
With my rattle I will say my prayers.
I pray for victory against my enemies.
Great Spirit, help me fight well!

My name is Washakie, the Rattler!
It is good,
My life will be good.

Because of the good luck they had with the hunt, the following day was proclaimed a day of feasting. The Chief announced they would also hold a council to decide what should be done about the ever-increasing menace of white men coming into their country to trap.

The council was held at night. The warriors assembled just outside the lodge of their Chief, who placed Washakie at his right hand in the seat of honor. Pah-da-hē-wa-kun-da grasped the young

man's hand and told him he wanted him to be his
son, to take the place of his own sons who had
been slain in battle with the Cheyennes and Sioux.
As his father, he wished to teach him all things that
would make him a good man and a fine warrior,
and he hoped that as time went on, Washakie
would merit a place in the council. Considering the
line of Flathead chieftains from whom his father,
Paseego, was descended, he thought it likely indeed
that Washakie would be found worthy. It was plain
that the old man's heart went out to Washakie.

The youth drew his talisman out of its beaded
pouch which he wore suspended about his neck.
Holding it in his hand, he accepted Pah-da-he-wa-
kun-da's offer to be his father:

"Surely, O Chief, my Medicine has guided my
footsteps to the Shoshones. You will be my father;
you will be even more, for you are not just a man,
you are a great leader."

Suddenly, Washakie felt a kinship for Pah-da-he-
wa-kun-da stronger than anything he had ever
experienced before. He felt the spirit of the Chief
reaching out to embrace his own. Drawing his knife

and puncturing the skin of his forearm, he dipped
his finger into his blood and marked a bright red line
upon the Chieftain's breast. Pah-da-he-wa-kun-da
likewise traced a sign with his blood upon the breast
of Washakie, who now became the Chief's blood
brother as well as his son—a bond that would
remain for the life of the two men. Washakie knew
that this was what he had wished and prayed for,
that he would be forever pledged in this strong
bond of brotherhood which could never be
loosened. He also knew that his life, henceforth,
would be dedicated to his mother's people, the
Eastern Shoshones.

All the councilors who were seated in the
circle, sensed the sacred covenant of that moment.
They were very still. The only movement was the
wavering flicker of the fire's reflections across the
quiet, intent faces. It lighted up the jewelry and
feathers and paint upon the warriors, and glittered
upon the tomahawks and metal armbands. To
Washakie it seemed that the swastika emblem on his
amulet glowed mysteriously. It glowed, even
though the stone upon which the emblem was

9

engraved was dull and dark. Unexpectedly, all warriors arose as one man and shouted his name, claiming him as their own: "Washakie, Shoshone!"

Then the councilors sat down to consider how to meet the white men who had come to trade with them, to exchange the Indians' furs for tools, guns, blankets, cloth and beads. After the chiefs had expressed their views upon the matter—most of them concurring that, while they should take advantage of the barter, they could always strike back with vengeance if the whites became troublesome—Washakie was given a chance to speak.

The young man told them that he had known Canadian trappers and trackers who treated the Indians well, and that some tribes had grown rich as a result. Why should not the Shoshones welcome them and likewise become wealthy? "Not all white men," he said, "are deceitful. We should give them at least a chance."

These trusting words were spoken at the conclusion of his forceful argument, and they agreed to abide by Washakie's plan. Thus, the Shoshones came in contact with Jim Bridger and started to exchange goods with the white men. Jim Bridger was a trapper, trader, and guide of high renoun among the mountain men of the Far West. In 1842, with his partner, Louis Vasquez, he established the first trading post ever built beyond the Mississippi. It was built to help immigrants and, indeed, marked the beginning of the era of immigration into the Far West.

The relationship between Washakie's Shoshones and Jim Bridger was to continue for many, many winters. In time, Jim Bridger married a daughter of Chief Washakie. The future seemed bright for the Shoshones, Washakie thought, and prosperity and peace would come in the footsteps of the trading, and the Great Spirit would be good to them.

In the days that followed, Washakie grew ever closer in all ways to Pah-da-he-wa-kun-da. Closer were they even than father and son. The old Chief taught him the ancient craft of governing a people, the art of discernment at the council fire, and the skills needed on the warpath.

Courtesy of the Uinta County Museum

Chapter 2
Bravest of the Brave

It was night when the Blackfeet raided the Shoshone camp. All were asleep. It was no trouble for the enemy to stampede every Shoshone horse. Several people were seized and taken captive, and among these was the Chief's granddaughter, Crimson Dawn.

Washakie was determined to be foremost among those desiring to retaliate. He went to Pah-da-he-wa-kun-da and offered to go on the warpath against the Blackfeet and take the scalp of every one of their warriors. He only needed some followers. They could get horses from other Indians in the nearby country, as well as extra recruits. Everyone approved the plan, and the men prepared for battle. Before leaving, Washakie pledged that he would find and return the Chief's granddaughter.

The warriors rode through the Old South Pass to Wind River Canyon, where the current had slashed a deep cavity into the earth. The war party had to go around this canyon; as yet no one had ever crossed it. After traversing the Owl Creek Mountains, they made camp and held council within sight of the peaks now called Washakie Needles.

The stars were bright in the sky when Washakie gave his last-minute instructions. He told the boys who had come on this, their first warpath as servants to the tried warriors, that when they came upon the Blackfeet, they had to ride among the horse herd, stampede it and drive it to the hills, there to hold it until the end of the battle.

Then, Washakie took out his war pipe. It was a combination pipe and tomahawk, the blade of steel, the shaft of copper. The pipe bowl was decorated with a picture of an Indian standing over his fallen foe. One side of the blade showed a charging group of warriors, the other a camp scene. This war pipe Washakie had won as a trophy in battle while still living with the Bannocks. It had originally come from some Northern tribe, who had gotten it in trade from the French. Now, the pipe was ceremoniously smoked by all, and prayers for their safety were said by the medicine man. Washakie began to speak. He punctuated his speech by

14

shaking his rattle, saying he did not intend to turn
back before victory was gained, no matter what
difficulties might lie ahead.

Again, they scouted the land for the enemy,
Washakie leading them. At last, they spotted the
Blackfeet, camped at the junction of Clark's Fork and
the Yellowstone River, the teepees spread on a flat,
with a river on either side. While scouts
reconnoitered the hills about, Washakie prayed for
success. Silent, was his rattle, now. It was to be his
first engagement in battle for the Shoshones, and he
prayed fervently that the Great Father would bring
honor to himself, his companions and his tribe. One
other prayer he added, and it was not for battle
glory, but that power might be granted to rescue
Crimson Dawn. She was a captive in that Blackfeet
camp. Ever since he had first seen this slender, dark-
haired beauty, wanted by so many of his fellow
warriors as their woman, he had cherished a secret
wish that some day she would be his. He had,
however, told no one; even his adopted father and
blood brother had not known of it until the Blackfeet
had captured her.

15

From a hilltop where he waited with his chief lieutenants in the first faint morning light, Washakie watched his direction being carried out. Silently his warriors rode down from the surrounding hills. He knew they held deadly arrows, strung, ready to be released. Washakie had commanded that the men be shot down, and the women be spared. It was all done, thus, before dawn, which such quiet precision that the Blackfeet were utterly surprised. For many of them there was hardly any time to get up from their sleep.

Then, on order of Washakie, more fighters galloped in the camp. Shoshone war cries rent the air. Before any Blackfeet could possibly escape, the Shoshones struck them down. Washakie himself led this final charge. His tomahawk dealt death everywhere. From one of his warriors he heard that Crimson Dawn was hidden in certain lodge. He made his way towards it, slaying as he went. He chose this particular time to rescue the girl, because he would be least noticed. About to dismount from his horse so that he could creep into the teepee, he was confronted the Head Chief of the Blackfeet who fought him like a mad bear; yet he was no match for the Shoshone. The Blackfeet Chieftain loosed an arrow at Washakie. The stone arrow point plowed a deep, bloody furrow into Washakie's left cheek, just under the eye, the scar of which he would carry all his life. Then, Washakie rode alongside the Chief. Both of them swung their tomahawks. Suddenly, with a swift lunge and a lightning stroke, Washakie clove the skull of the Blackfeet.

After ending the life of the enemy leader, Washakie immediately went back towards the lodge where Crimson Dawn was hidden. But the teepee had been wrecked and lay turned upside down. He lifted the cover and found her, at last, lying helplessly bound hand and foot. Quickly, he cut her bond. She recognized him, and in wordless gratitude, put her arms around his neck. He carried her to the safest place he could find, among a group of Blackfeet women and children who had been spared.

Those Blackfeet who had the good fortune not to be killed—and they were mostly women, children, and old people—began to look after their many dead. The bodies were laid upon platforms, and placed high in the branches of trees up high, to protect them from wild animals and other trespassers. The bodies were dressed in their best clothing and were surrounded with cherished possessions, so their spirits would arrive happy at the Hereafter that they called Sand Hills. Some slain warriors were left in lonely lodges that had not been destroyed by enemy, to be gradually destroyed by the elements. Still more bodies were buried under piles of stones, buried just where they had fallen. The place of burial and destruction resounded with the pitiful cries and wails of the mourners.

Few had been killed among the Shoshones, although many had been wounded. Washakie made sure that all of them were well cared for. The great quantity of loot which the victorious Shoshones had taken from the enemy camp was divided equally among the warriors. Washakie checked on the impartial treatment of every one in his party. He kept for himself only the weapon and other belongings of the Blackfeet Chieftain he had slain.

Astride his Bannock pinto cayuse, which had carried him so well in the battle, he led his triumphant group homeward. They took the shortest route across the Owl Creek Mountains and, continuing south, along the foothills of what white man called the Rocky Mountains, and back over the South Pass. All hearts were beating with pride at the manner in which Washakie had performed on his first warpath with the Shoshones. His own heart was not only overflowing with gratitude over his success, but it was filled with love for Crimson Dawn. She followed far behind, in the cavalcade of homeward-bound travelers, accompanied by two Blackfeet women.

For a while, Washakie found no chance as they traveled to catch even a glimpse of the girl that he loved. Then, in a wild glen at South Pass, he called a halt to the march and sought her out. It was done so secretly that even the woman who guarded her did not see her slip away. The words she had not said to Washakie when he had rescued her were now sweetly uttered. They found they had great love for one another.

"This is even better than stealing you from your father's lodge," he said to her, referring to the Shoshone marriage custom of a man stealing his sweetheart from the family teepee and making off with her, "and for you, also, my Love, I thank Dama Uppa."

19

When the war party arrived at their camp, the old Chieftain embraced his granddaughter, in silent thanksgiving. Then, aloud, he praised Washakie for his fine leadership in battle. Before all the people he now proclaimed that his granddaughter, Crimson Dawn, should become the wife of the young warrior. And Pah-de-he-wa-kun-da announced that when evening came they would celebrate their triumphant victory over their enemies with a feast and athletic competition.

Painting by Ralph Tillman

After nightfall, when the feasting and competition was over, the Victory Dance took place, when the warriors vividly and dramatically acted out their deeds in battle, in pantomime. At one moment, the crowd would hold its breath at other times they yell with fury. Washakie, at the request of the Chief, related the tale of victory, with his great mastery of words. Washakie's Medicine surely had found favor with the Great Father of ALL. He was not only an orator, but also an accomplished diplomat. He described the cunning and skill of his warriors in fighting; he took time, also, to praise his adopted father's teaching in battle lore. When telling of the encounter with the Blackfeet, Washakie looked every inch a Chieftain, his face and bearing striking awe in his listeners.

Pah-da-he-wa-kun-da called Washakie over to him. The latter sat down beside the Chief, in the Chief's teepee, and waited for him to speak.

"For my Son and Brother," began the Shoshone leader, "these are important words. Listen well! There is a destiny for Washakie that was planned a very long time ago, before he was born. This will be a changing world, and Washakie will see how the white man will rule supreme over all. Never again will the Indian be free as he has been, for the white man's greed will take all that has belonged to the Indian. This, Washakie must meet unafraid. It is for Washakie, the Chosen One, to fulfill the hope and trust that have been placed in him. His goals will be reached through danger and toil. It will take much courage. A free conscience must he have, faith in himself, and good works must he do to all men. The whole of a man's possessions—his horses, robes, teepee, everything fine he owns—these Washakie will forsake. What the great father, Dama Uppa, gives him, he will share with others, keeping nothing for himself. Even though things that make a man happy, such as his frame as a warrior in battle, Washakie will forego. For the sake of peace for all men, he will shun war. Henceforth he must follow the Peaceful Path. He will find, however, that the Great Father of All will bestow on him the gift of peace to his own spirit, and will likewise grant him the gifts of strength and goodness and generosity, and knowledge of all things true. Possession of these will make Washakie the bravest of the brave warriors."

Pah-da-he-wa-kun-da looked the young man squarely in the eyes, and it seemed to Washakie that the brilliant, fathomless eyes of the old Chief penetrated deep inside of him, and were speaking to his very spirit.

"A journey must my son take, to the Medicine Wheel," the Chief continued, "At this sacred place will my Son learn, and be shown Truth and the way to live with his fellow men. This will fit him for his life's service to his brother. He must take the Path chosen for him. The talisman that he wears on his breast means that he must tread the path which I, Pah-da-he-wa-kun-da, have trod, and which the Flathead Chieftain who gave the talisman to Washakie, at his birth, also trod...Do go, my Son, to the Medicine Wheel."

Washakie took his rattle and chanted, softly to himself:

The Talisman,
My Medicine,
Will lead me aright!

23

I shall tread
The Unknown Way
With courage.
With courage
Will I tread it!

Dama Uppa*
And my Medicine
Will show me the Way!

He spent that night in a quiet, solitary place, praying, singing, and thinking of the Path that he must follow. He would shake his rattle and chant his prayers.

* Dama Uppa, also spelled *Tamapah,* is Shoshone for Sun-Father of the Day, and Father of Us All, who lives in the sun. The name Great Spirit mentioned in this story is identical in meaning with Dama Uppa, Father of Us All, or God.

Chapter 3
Journey to
the Medicine Wheel

In the morning Washakie said farewell to Pah-
da-he-wa-kun-da and his people, and started on his
way to the Medicine Wheel. It was located far in the
North, in the country of the Crow Indians, at the
upper end of the Big Horn Mountain Range.
Medicine was wrought there upon a mountain top;
truth was taught there by ancient men, pure and
wise. Washakie could only hope that the Great
Father of All would favor his desire to become a
member in the Sacred Brotherhood of Man. Once
there at the Wheel, he would have to display his
talisman to the Ancient Ones and give them a certain
Word, which the old Chief had entrusted to him.

For the journey he took bow and arrows, two
pair of moccasins, and kinnikinnick to smoke in his
pipe. He wore only a plain leather shirt and leggings,
unembellished, upon his tall, strong body. A single

feather decked his hair, and he carried his talisman
over his heart. And, naturally, he took with him his
rattle and his tomahawk.

It was not long before he came upon a
Cheyenne camp, located upon the plain, in the
vicinity of Gooseberry Creek, which is not far from
the Big Horn Mountains in what is now upper
Wyoming. Washakie determined to make a lone raid
upon the horses. He reasoned that he did not want
the ponies for himself; that would go against the
promise he had made not to take to himself
possessions. However, he did need a better horse for
riding, as his own was worn out and not sufficiently
fast. It was a necessity to get another horse, now.
Still, this was to be his last raid for his personal gain.

Hiding in a deep coulee, he watched the
animals. He wished to take a horse without harming
anyone in the camp. Toward midnight, he started to
approach the pony herd. The shaking of his rattle
caused the horses to stampede, and he followed
them at full speed. Finally, he had driven the horses
far enough away from the camp, and could rest. He
had noticed that the herd was led by a huge, red
roan, with wonderful speed. Ah, that was the horse

for him! It had a mane like flowing silver moonlight. This animal would have the stamina and swiftness to carry him far. He captured the horse in a short while, mounted it, and sped away towards the north.

In the future at many a home camp fire, this tale of Washakie's lone horse raid would be told. And from this time on, Washakie was called "The Rattler" also by his enemies, for when forced to it, he struck, quick and deadly, as the snake; indeed, more deadly, for he gave no warning at all.

He entered the Big Horn Range, in the country of the Crow Indians. His great horse carried him well. The trail was hard and wearisome. He prayed earnestly that he might reach his destination. Then, one day he saw the mountain upon whose flattened top was the Medicine Wheel. When he had arrived at its base, he was met by an old man at least one hundred winters of age, who seemed to float rather than walk. He must have seemed hardly human. When Washakie showed him the talisman, however, he smiled broadly, and the ragged smile with scarcely a tooth visible was human enough.

He offered to guide the young Shoshone up the mountain, and together they went through a hidden valley, and up a precipitous path leading straight to the top. Mysterious mists enfolded everything, making progress difficult. They had to watch for fallen rocks and other obstructions. The trail steepened sharply when they neared the summit. It looked as though the old guide had superhuman strength, because he led the way upward so easily and surely.

Painting by Ralph Tillman

View near the Great Immigration and Mormon Trails where Chief Washakie saved many lives.

When they reached the place of the Wheel, Washakie saw that it was built of stones, the spokes of the wheel being straight and of perfect symmetry. He counted seven of these giant spokes; in between them smaller spokes, making a total of twenty-eight. At the center or hub of the Wheel was a large altar while four smaller altars, each one composed of a pile of stones, were located at the four quarters, North, South, East, and West. On the outside of the Wheel was a path, forming a complete square, beaten there by the feet of many pilgrims come to pay homage through the ages. Washakie knew that the origin of this Wheel stretched beyond the memory of any of the Indian tribes.

He spent that night in prayer.

As the sun began to rise, he approached the Wheel and stepped naked before the huge center altar. He was told to kneel and pray to the Great Spirit. Might all the future winters of his life be full of strong faith! Might power be granted him to do what was good and true and righteous!

A patriarch, a man of incredible age, with a long, flowing beard and blue eyes, and wearing a white robe, approached him as he knelt praying.

"Who is this, who dares to come to the Sacred Wheel?" the Old One asked, in a surprisingly strong, resonant voice.

"A Shoshone youth, come to learn the way of Truth," was the reply.

"A sign? A token?"

Washakie showed his talisman.

"It carries the signs of truth," started the Patriarch. "It was once the property of a Flathead Chief, who was a leader of men."

Then, Washakie spoke the Sacred Password which Pah-da-he-wa-kun-da had given him, and the Patriarch disclosed to him the sacred things he must know. He mentioned the one true God that all men must worship, and explained that there is life after death and that spirit continues on. Now, for the remainder of his years, Washakie must live a good life, according to the way of Truth, and if he wished to be part of the great Brotherhood, he had to promise obedience to his superiors, the noble leaders. He was informed that there was a Chieftain in every Northern Indian tribe who, together with his

medicine men, had pledged himself within the
Sacred Wheel to trust his fellow men and to serve
one God. Washakie then was told that his next
assignment would be to go to a land where he
would find material for making a Pipe of Peace.
When he returned with his completed peace pipe,
the final rites within the Wheel and the Brotherhood
would be accorded to him.

> O sacred smoke, ascending
> From the Pipe of Peace,
> Make the Almighty listen
> To the prayers of men,
>
> For safety, mercy, healing
> Peace to all the tribes.
> To helpful spirits, appealing,
> Smoke, rising up to heaven.

So Washakie started on his way to Pipestone
Land, where lived the hostile Sioux Indians, far to the
East, close to where later the states of South Dakota
and Minnesota would share a border. Somewhere

along the trail, he came across a white trapper and
ate of his food. He felt confidence in this man and
asked to travel with him. After days, they reached the
camp of the Mandan Indians, and shortly thereafter
they found a welcome at the nearby white man's fort
located north of the present town of Bismarck, North
Dakota. Here they met a French interpreter named
Charbonneau whose Shoshone wife, Sacajawea,
told them about the long journey she had taken
many winters past (about 1805) guiding a party of
white men, the leaders of which were Lewis and
Clark. So vividly did she describe her experiences,
that Washakie could see in his mind the great
Western ocean and the big fish they called whales.

Resuming his trek southeastward to the
Pipestone country, Washakie fell in with a Pawnee
warrior, also going to get pipestone. The Shoshone
learned that their missions were somewhat similar,
and they soon became fast friends, and traveled
together. Sometimes at night sitting by the campfire
Washakie would tell the Pawnee about Sacajawea
and how it had warmed him to see a woman willing
to help her fellow men. Even though the strangers

she helped might have a different color of skin and a different way of living, she gave of her great heart and of her courage. Her name would by honored by white men and Indians alike.

Later, Washakie and the Pawnee were guests of another tribe of Indians, and they were entertained at a feast where Washakie recounted his saga of the Blackfeet battle in which he had won his honors. His host gave him directions where to find the red stone

Courtesy of Wyoming Division of Cultural Resources

The Medicine Wheel located in the Big Horn
Mountains of Wyoming. This site is a sacred landmark
for all Native Americans.

with which to make their pipes. Soon, they reached the quarries and dug out an ample supply of the catlinite, which was soft enough when freshly cut to be carved into a pipe bowl. Great Chiefs and warriors of ages past had obtained their pipe material from this place, long revered and traditionally held neutral for all tribes.

Now the time came for Washakie and the Pawnee to part company, for they had to travel different routes. They exchanged gifts. Washakie received a pair of gloves, and in turn gave a fine arrow to his companion. At the middle of the Cold Moon (December) he returned to the Mandan fort. By this time Charbonneau had died and had left Sacajawea with two children to care for. She asked that she might go back with Washakie to her own Shoshone people, and he consented gladly. After a while they met white trappers who were trading with the Black Hills Indians. Washakie agreed to scout and hunt for them, so he and Sacajawea remained there until Spring. Then, the two traveled West until they came to the Powder River, after which they turned southward, following the river valley. There, Washakie told Sacajawea he must leave

her for a brief period. It was for an important reason.
He would come back for her as soon as possible,
and she should wait for him at the river.

When at last he arrived back at the Wheel, he
learned that the Patriarch had passed on, several
moons past. The wise man who had guided him up
the mountain was near death himself. Washakie
feared that he would never receive any further
instructions or help and felt in his deep sorrow that
he, too, would die. The old man, however, with
glazing eyes, looked up at him, and began to speak.

"I give you the Word of the Sacred Cult of the
Wheel," the wise man whispered, hoarsely. "All
brothers...receive this word. Use it....well...always.
Always...use it for good...for others. For others...live."

"Tell me, what is the Word, O my father?" asked
Washakie.

"It is..." The Wise One paused, unable to
continue. Finally, however, he managed to breathe a
three-syllable word. Washakie knew the word was
extremely sacred.

"Yes, my Father!" he said eagerly. "It will be used
always for good, and always to help all men. This
Washakie promises."

The aged man started to tell him something else, but death caught him before the words could pass from his lips, even though Washakie bent his ear very close.

Alone then Washakie made his way down the mountain, leaving the Place of the Wheel. Never could he now learn the remainder of the message and the truths of the Wheel, he thought; still, he could help spread the light of Truth, the knowledge of the Fatherhood of God, and the Brotherhood of Men. He knew enough to do this. He, Washakie, would strive to lead the Shoshones henceforth in the best way he knew. Always, would he follow the precepts laid down for him by the Brotherhood.

Chapter 4
Leadership

When Washakie reached the Powder River again, he found Sacajewea waiting for him, and the woman guide of Lewis and Clark now led him towards home. She remembered the land of her childhood well. At last Fremont's Lake came into view, and there they saw encamped a small division of the Shoshone people. The Chief of this band of about one hundred men and their woman and children was Norkuk. Sacajawea was overjoyed to find among them, Basil, her nephew, who later became her adopted son

That evening the pipe was passed around the circle of men sitting around the council fire. Washakie asked after the whereabouts of Pah-da-he-wa-kun-da. Norkuk informed him the Chief had died during the past winter's snows and that his people were now disorganized and scattered.

Washakie heard the news with sadness. He spoke quietly at first, recounting how his adopted father had been such a wise counselor to him. But now, his voice sounded strong and firm, it was time that the Shoshones raise themselves to greater glory. To become united and secure, they must rebuild the faith in their tribal eminence. Washakie wished to pledge his own life to this end. He invited all Shoshones to do likewise, to regather the whole tribe, and to accept the vow to live forever in one brotherhood.

Basil, who was to become Chief Medicine Man, proposed that Washakie be accepted as their Chieftain, to be followed to the death. Together, the council arose. Each man drew his knife across his arm and touched his blood to the breast of Washakie; the latter in return touched each councilor with his own blood. Thus they pledged their loyalty, not only to Washakie as the supreme leader, but also to the strength and betterment of the Shoshone tribe in days to come.

After Washakie was made Head Chief, the people wanted to hear of his recent travels. He told them about his raid on the Cheyenne pony herd; his exploits with the Sioux; his Pawnee friend; his stay at the Mandan trading post; and the lone trapper whose food he had shared. Only his visit to the Medicine Wheel did he keep secret, for he could not tell the sacred things that had been revealed to him there.

At the conclusion of his account of his adventures, he returned to the subject of his selection as Head Chief. He declared that he accepted the responsibility, but emphasized he would demand strict obedience of every member of the Shoshones. At the council fire the councilors would help decide the actions of the tribe; but in battle or on the march his will was to be law. Each one must promptly fulfill his every command. He would be true to all Indian laws, adhere to all customs of the people and defend their rights. When white men appeared the Shoshones would keep the peace, although they would never be slaves to them. They had to grow strong and content. Let couriers be sent to all other Shoshones, asking cooperation and requesting them to follow Washakie.

Norkuk and Basil told Washakie that white trappers gave the young warriors whiskey, so that

their laziness and evil doings were the shame of their
people. They had become wild, as the wild horses
that ranged the hillsides. They roved lawlessly, in
small bands. Some of the youths had joined the
Bannocks; other delighted in loafing around the
trading posts. The only persons who held the tribe
together and kept the laws were the older ones.
These older ones hoped for better days. At present, a
group of these older, responsible men were gathered
to spend the summer in the Grand Teton Range. In
fact, Norkuk's band was at this time planning to go
there.

Washakie agreed that they should join them. It
would be a demanding task to surmount the
difficulties before them of lawless young men, white
man's whiskey, and Indian foes. They would, as a
tribe, retain their old-time hunting grounds and
return to spend the winters by the Green River. Here
the mountains on the East and West would shelter
them from their enemies.

When Norkuk's group arrived at the Grand
Tetons, they set up camp with some Shoshones
already there, upon the bank of a clear lake, pine-

fringed, whose blue waters reflected the clouds and
the mountains rising above it. The snow-capped
peaks were shaped like sharp teeth, jagged, awe-
inspiring. High in the center of the peaks stood one
majestic cone, with a white snow-glacier running
down its side that shone in the sun. The lake was
later to be called by white settlers Jackson Lake, and
the imposing mountain, standing like a sentinel
eternal, Mount Moran. This unforgettable country
was still later to be made into one of the most
beautiful playgrounds of the white man's nation.
Shoshone country it was, at the time of Washakie;
and Shoshone country it was always to remain.

Washakie was amazed and enthralled by the
grandeur of this land around him, and he felt that
indeed it was the right place to hold important Tribal
Councils. This place would inspire them to lofty ideals
and help them always make the best and wisest of
decisions. This setting seemed to Washakie to be also
a perfect one for a wedding. Here, he would unite
himself with Crimson Dawn. Although he head was
filled with the ambitions and cares of his tribe she
should wait no longer. After the celebration he
would call the council.

Shoshone marriage custom demanded that the man go to the lodge of the girl, call her out, seize her, and carry her to his own teepee. So, when evening came and the moon had risen full over Mount Moran and the lake covering everything with its silver light, Washakie stepped up to Crimson Dawn's lodge and stood in front of it.

"Crimson Dawn!" he called her name loudly.

The girl inside the lodge scrambled to her feet. She knew what was happening, she had been waiting for this moment; she was, nevertheless, excited and pretended surprise. Her two women companions tried unsuccessfully to prevent her from running out. She flew into Washakie's arms and he lifted her up and carried her off to his teepee. At long last, the two lovers were united in the love of man and wife! Washakie thought as he made love to his woman, that now his life held all it could contain. He knew what he must do for his people; his path was marked out for him to follow. He had a goal for his future. Not least, he had the perfect love of a woman, and he was a complete man.

At rise of sun excitement filled the whole camp, as preparations for the wedding festivities began.

Painting by Ralph Tillman

Location of marriage of Washakie and Crimson Dawn, near
present day Jackson Lake, Wyoming

Many of their own Shoshone people and visitors from other tribes arrived to witness the celebration. That evening there was feasting and dancing, and at the end, a portrayal in pantomime of the love of Washakie for Crimson Dawn and her rescue from the Blackfeet.

After the wedding celebration and a short period of rest, Washakie called the council to assemble. He was his own announcer walking around the camp shouting out the news of the gathering in a resounding voice.

Those who had come for the wedding stayed on, so the camp remained a large one. Among those present at the council were all those wise and older men of the tribe, including Norkuk and his leaders. They assembled in a wide circle on the green grass beside the lake. The air, fresh and vibrant, inspired to new life and anticipation. Washakie looked upward at the impressive mountain with the white snow-glacier upon it.

"That mountain," he said, "makes me feel big, and able to do big things in my life. I know that all of you feel the same. I know also that we Shoshones will be able with the help of the Great Father of All to make our tribe strong. Let us begin our council, then, by talking about what we must do to help all of us. One of the most important tasks will be to rid our people of the whiskey that the white men push on us. They cannot, they must not, press this evil upon us any longer. We will make this our first objective: resist the crazy drink which saps the strength and minds of our young men and weakens us so much. The drink must be denied to every one of us, too. Those who drink must suffer punishment. Norkuk, let me have your ideas and opinions upon this matter."

So, on this, and other subjects concerning Shoshones' welfare, Norkuk and the other leaders deliberated. The council terminated that day with many sound decisions made. Great Father did, indeed, make a wise and good beginning for the government of Washakie's Shoshones!

*　*　*　*

For sixty winters more Chief Washakie remained the Shoshones' only Head Chieftain. He ruled as a despot, but he was, all the same, kind and

honest. He gave himself fully in service to the tribe.
Feeling the needs of his people and putting himself
in their places, he was just in all his judgments. The
guilty were punished, the good rewarded. From
scattered bands, he gradually built one large closely
knit tribe. Only in defense did he fight against hostile
tribes, such as Arapahoes, Cheyennes, Sioux, and
Crows, who insisted upon encroaching upon his
peoples' rights and territory. He was victorious in his
battles. Skillful in war and wise in peace, Washakie
ruled.

To all white men, he proved a great support. To
Kit Carson, and all other mountain men and
trappers, who crossed his territory, he showed
kindness and fairness, seeking both harmony and
understanding with them. He sought fairness, too,
with the white traders at their trading posts. He did
not harm immigrants who crossed his country,
letting them travel in peace.

Washakie was far-seeing, however, and realized
he must do something to save his tribe from the
threatening deluge of white settlers, who came into
his country. A terrible craze for gold was consuming

settlers and greed for that yellow metal that they dug out of Mother Earth was driving all else before it. Shoshones were puzzled by this avarice which caused ill-will, trickery, and bloodshed, but they were well-counseled and strictly kept in check by their leader.

Nevertheless, Indian wisdom could not hold its own against the more powerful white man's skills. Bow and arrow and war club could not compete with guns. The time would soon be at hand when game would disappear from the land, through the ruthlessness, selfishness and foolishness of white hunters. Then, the Shoshones would not have sufficient food or shelter unless they kept their own lands and started to raise crops, giving in to the white man's urging to do farming. Farming must some day provide the answer to the problem of the Indians' survival. Washakie knew that no one would like this solution.

The Latter Day Saints, popularly called Mormons, or 'Saints', arrived in Utah Territory in 1847. They had been run out of the state of Illinois because of their religious beliefs and had gone west

to Utah to find a home there. As they traveled to
Utah, via the Oregon Trail, they found they did not
have to fear attack by Shoshone Indians. They were
attacked by other Indians but not by Shoshones who
let them travel in peace. After settling in Utah, the
Saints developed a warm and mutually helpful
relationship with Washakie's Shoshones. The leader
of the Saints, Brigham Young, became a good friend
to Chief Washakie. While other Indian tribes savagely
resisted the onrush of whites, Shoshones, under their
Chief's guidance, kept peace and cooperation in
every way with Brigham Young's people.

Then, by 1857, after ten winters and a long
friendship with the Saints, Washakie began to see
how so very much Shoshone land was being taken,
stolen, by those good friends of his! The Saints had
already taken over all Shoshone land in Wyoming
Territory, and land in Idaho, also. It bothered the
Chief, too, to see how those people were settling
around Green River, those good hunting lands the
Shoshones frequented, thinking of it as their home.
More than others, Washakie considered that country
his home, for his friend Jim Bridger had built a fort

there and carried on a good trading business with the Indians, as well as with whites, and had married the Chief's daughter, Mary. Washakie was happy with this alliance and content with his life at Green River.

Then in 1853 a terrible thing happened to Jim Bridger. The Saints had asked Bridger to give them his trading fort, but Bridger had refused. The Saints came and took over Fort Bridger by force. Bridger became a fugitive, fearful of the Mormons and eventually took his family to Missouri to live.

Shortly thereafter, in 1857 though, the U.S. government noticed the greedy actions of the Saints who were illegally taking over Indian land. A military force was sent against the Saints in Utah after they announced they would secede from the United States. Chief Washakie was asked to aid in fighting the Saints, and he accepted. He offered 1,200 of his warriors to help the Army fight the people of Brigham Young, who were now his enemies.

Shoshones lost many warriors in this "Mormon War," (1857-58). In all, about four hundred were killed. When the fight was over, the United States and the Shoshone Tribe had won and had driven the Saints back into Utah. Chief Washakie rejoiced and thanked Dama Uppa that he had defended and saved his peoples' lands from the clutches of a group he saw as greedy thieves. Another battle had been won for his tribe, and this victory showed white men that they could not just take Indians' land that did not belong to them. This victory showed whites that they must honor treaties with the Indians.

Chapter 5
The Trials of Leadership

Washakie's wife, the beautiful Crimson Dawn, had died giving birth to their son, whom they had called Nau-nang-gai. This son grew up to be a young warrior. One day the Sioux raided the Shoshones camp. Washakie the warrior was ready to ride out to battle, but he did not see his son among the warriors. When Washakie returned from the fight, bringing with him many scalps, the first thing he did was to seek Nau-nang-gai. Just then, the young man was entering camp, coming back from the white man's settlement with other pleasure-seeking young men. They were happy, carefree, and some were drunk. The drinking alone was enough to evoke in their Chieftain a passionate rage, so he was furiously angry. The dangerous quality of his anger, when fully aroused, was well known to his people. At such time his temper was something to be avoided! The Chief came out of his lodge and approached the young men. They scattered like prairie chickens. Washakie had the camp policemen catch them and place them in a prison teepee for an uncomfortable stay. As for Nau-nang-gai, had the youth not inherited from his illustrious father that same courage in the face of great odds, he, also, would have tried to flee. However, he faced his father. The Chief lashed out at him.

"My son is a sulking coward! He who did not enter the fight is not fit to be my son!"

The boy stood, motionless, bitterly stung by the harsh words, since he had asked permission from his father to be absent, even before the Sioux had attacked their camp.

"Be a credit to your people, or return not to your father," were Washakie's last words to him, and Nau-nang-gai turned, flung himself on his horse and disappeared from sight.

It was not long after that a messenger rode into camp with news that Nau-nang-gai was no more. He had been so indignant and hurt by his father's words, that he had charged wildly into the Sioux with no concern for his safety. He had killed even more of the enemy warriors than had Washakie himself.

The father was stricken with grief, to such an extent that he requested to be left alone with the mutilated body of his son when it was brought into camp, and he fasted for nearly four days thereafter. The great Chief's hair turned white overnight, as he mourned Nau-nang-gai. His friends and family thought he also would die. Never did he get over the death of his son, for which he knew he had been responsible. His only solace in his sorrow was hard work and the cares of his tribe. His iron will and rule over the Shoshones became firmer still, but at the same time his stern methods prevented much potential trouble. The young men always knew that Washakie was master of every situation.

The beginning of the 1860s brought the Civil War to the white people in the East, but it did not affect the lives of the Shoshones.

The time arrived when representatives of the Washington government came to discuss placing the Shoshone Tribe on land that would be theirs for all time. Washakie agreed to this, on condition that he could choose the country of his heart's desire, the Wind River Valley, in what is now Wyoming. It was called the 'Warm Valley' because of the mild winds, called *chinooks* that often blew down from mountains and melted the snows of winter, bringing a temporary warmth that was almost spring-like. Close proximity to the high mountains kept it cool in summer. Chief Washakie selected the valley for his own. Of all the ranges in the great Rocky Mountain chain, the Wind River Mountains—with the possible exception of the mountain peaks the white man had named Tetons—were unsurpassed in beauty. There was the lovely North Fork. There was the breath-taking scene at the mouth of the South Fork of Wind River, with its towering fortress-like gateway leading into the canyon, the misty, far-reaches of the mountains beyond, blending into the great snow-capped heights above.

The soil of the valley was rich, good for farming and raising cattle, as the government men encouraged them to do. Moreover, all kinds of game were plentiful. Buffalo roamed even to the base of the foothills. Assuredly this was the country for the Shoshones to have and to hold!

Washakie felt he must wait, however, before leading his people into the paradise he had chosen because hostile tribes hunted that rich land. To live there in safety his people would need protection. He asked that the government build a fort to provide some protection. It became a disappointing delay of many winters, as the Shoshones remained by the Green River, while the U.S. government made no move to build the fort.

The move to the Wind River Valley was also delayed because of the discovery of gold in the valley, which caused many white settlers and prospectors flock into the valley. The greed and complacency of these people would not let them give up the land they had taken. Squatters coveted the rich farmlands and meant to keep and enlarge their holdings. Cattle began to take the place of buffalo. Small settlements began to dot the land. The prospectors' greed was taking over Washakie's Warm Valley. What room would this leave for his Shoshone people?

As moons waxed and waned, Washakie grew older. He governed his people, however, with as firm a hand as ever. He remained a strong man physically also in spite of many snows and white hair. Still, this did not help him in the opinion of some of the younger tribesmen who grumbled that his leadership, while good in ways of peace, was sadly lacking in warlike qualities. At last, a group of plotters decided to put another leader in his place. Washakie discovered the conspiracy, however. It hurt his pride. Without telling anyone of his plan, he left camp and did not return for two moons. When he did return, he called a council. He summoned together the discontented ones as well as those who had plotted against him. They formed a circle about the council fire, waiting for him to speak.

He filled the bowl of his pipe with kinnikinnick, passing it around to the warriors. This pipe was the same one—half pipe and half weapon, with the bowl and blade engraved—the very one Washakie had made them smoke when first he led them to war against the Blackfeet. Now, the pipe was smoked reverently and in silence. Whenever people smoke it, they felt respect for it and for Washakie and his power of leadership. After each had his turn, Washakie spoke to them. His eyes flashed the old fire, and his voice was steady.

"I, Washakie, am your chief! I say to you that I shall always be your chief!"

He looked around the crowd, which seemed to shrink.

"Who will dare to deny this? Only some striplings with no brains and weak arms."

He pointed a rigid arm at the conspirators.

"You, and you, think I am an old man. Today, I will prove that I am not. You thought by trickery you

Courtesy of Wyoming Division of Cultural Resources

Crowheart Butte, Wyoming. Scene of the
Crow-Shoshone Battle

could dishonor an old man. Today, I will prove this. I put you in your place. Obey me, and you will live; disobey, and you die! I have always loved this justice and striven for good. My Medicine"— and his voice dropped its warlike tone at the words— "has always guided me aright to do the fair and correct thing for my people. I am a peaceful whenever possible, yet when battle is necessary, all my heart and spirit are in it. I will always wear upon my face a scar given me by the arrow of a Blackfeet. My son, my dear son, was slain in battle with the Sioux. My own father died honorably in battle."

Now, his magnificent voice rose again. "I will prove that I still have the arm and heart of a young man, though my hair is white."

With these words, he cast before them seven enemy scalps.

"Let those who cannot hope to emulate the deeds of Washakie in war or peace, forever silence keep. Let him be Chief who dares, alone and single-handed, to strike the enemy!"

The young plotters fled the council. After the confusion had died away Basil chose the ensuing quiet to speak the remaining warriors. After Basil,

Norkuk spoke. Norkuk said that for thirty winters they had followed Washakie. His Medicine was good; he lived for peace, yet no one was a greater warrior when it was demanded. Nobody could exceed him in this regard. He was the only one, also, who could combat the white man's deceit. The Shoshone always received their fair share of the rations when these were distributed. Any designs the white agent might have to give their people less than was due them or to foist off on them things of bad quality, or cheat them, were quickly discerned by the Chief. He accepted nothing less than the best for his people. If lands were given the Shoshones with the understanding that these would be theirs for all time, then Washakie made the white men keep their word. Let Washakie, then, be Chief!

The council arose, together, acclaiming Washakie. He acknowledged it quietly, warning them, however, that in future years they would not go to war nor even hunt as they had been used to do. They could not prevent the coming of the white man, so they had to learn to live with him, in his mode of life, and till the soil.

Thus, for the rest of his life, Washakie was to be Head Chieftain of the Shoshones. And never again was his leadership challenged.

*   *   *   *

In 1866, there was a battle between the Shoshones and Bannocks on one side and the Crows on the other. Washakie had sent a peace envoy to the Crows, a man and his wife. When only the woman came back with the news that the Crows had murdered her husband, the Shoshones decided on war and engaged the Bannocks to aid them. For four days they fought near what is now called Crowheart Butte, near Black Mountain.

> Up from Wyoming plain arising
> Stern sentinel, Crowheart Butte
> Under Black Mountain.

The battle was a terrible one, many warriors dying on either side. The Crows were at a disadvantage, since they were stranded in a spot where there was no water. At last the Crow Chief, Big Robber, challenged Chief Washakie to a duel. This promised to be a bitter contest, for the two

leaders were great enemies. It would decide the fate
of the entire battle. Whoever would win would
claim victory for his tribe.

Big Robber was armed with a lance. Washakie
rode up on him, wielding his long cavalry saber. It
was shorter than the Crow's lance; still, he used it
cleverly against his foe. The Crows were lined up on
one side of the dueling area, tensely watching; the
Shoshones and Bannocks were silently grouped on
the other.

Crow and Shoshone tribes assembled. . .
One can hear their war cries yet!
Big Robber with his lance attacking,
Washakie with his sword.

Finally, in spite of the handicap of his shorter
weapon, Washakie slew Big Robber. The Crow
warriors in desperation, turned to flee, but they were
cut off by the Shoshones.

It was admiration, not contempt for the valiant
Chief of the Crows, that made Washakie cut out the
heart of his opponent and later display it upon his

lance during the Shoshones' Victory Dance. Their
conquest gave the Shoshones undisputed title to the
Wind River Valley.

> Always may it be remembered,
> Never more brave fighters met
> On the field of battle, dueling,
> A Crow's heart
> As a banner waved,
> And for Washakie
> The Valley.

A particular and personal prize for Chief
Washakie was a little girl whom they called Aha-
waipu (Crow Woman), and who later became his
wife. She had been left behind with the Crow
lodges when the remainder of the vanquished
enemy had fled the territory.

Chapter 6
Washakie's Homecoming

An important treaty with the white man was signed in 1868, but again, nothing was done to carry out its terms. The Shoshones were left to live as they had for many winters—beside the Green

Chief Washakie and his granddaughter

River. Eventually, a fort was constructed in the Wind River Valley and troops occupied it. After the construction, Washakie was assured he could expect protection against the Sioux enemy tribe that had been harassing him, and the U.S. government would furnish him and his tribe with all the supplies they would need. A sawmill and a gristmill were built, a schoolhouse for the education of the Shoshone children was erected, and soon water was available to irrigate the farm land. The tribesmen were given cattle and horses. So, at last, Washakie was satisfied that his people's needs were being satisfied, and he led his tribe to his chosen land, to reside there permanently.

It was a long cavalcade that traversed the plain into the beautiful valley of Wind River. A band of warriors rode ahead as vanguard, Washakie and his chiefs at their head. Then followed the women and children, some walking, others riding the horses that pulled the heavily laden travois, those Indian transport devices made by stretching hides between two trailing poles. Children played noisily along the route. Boys amused themselves by racing each other on horseback. A rear guard, composed of old men, youths and some more seasoned warriors, came last.

From now on Washakie's principal aim in life was helping the members of his tribe to accustom themselves to getting along with the white man, and adopting such white ways that he could see helped them, while, at the same time, keeping and never forgetting their good old time ways that were part of their heritage, that made them a proud Shoshone tribe. The Chief was getting along in age—he counted nearly seventy-three winters—yet he was youthful and his mind keen to all things. His people listened to his advice, and began to till the fields and send their children to school. Slowly but surely, the Shoshones were leaving their ancient customs behind. Some built cabins for themselves, while others chose to live in tents or teepees, as their fathers had done. Some wished to learn all they could; others resented the changes. For all of them, it was hard to accustom themselves to the strangeness of their new lives. Washakie would say to them, "Take heart, it is for the best. We must do this." He tried hard to make them understand how it was necessary now for them.

Even though he continued to urge his fellow tribesmen to cooperate with the whites and accept things as they had become, he felt some secret anger and frustration with the realization that the white man's government was not keeping all the terms of the treaty signed in 1868 at Fort Bridger, which was part of the Utah territory at that time.

The land given the Shoshones in the 1868 treaty was steadily shrinking in size as more and more whites settled on the best lands. Washakie hated the agreement his people had been obliged to accept because it gave whites the areas containing oil and gold. The promised fort, named Fort Brown, had finally been built for protection against enemy tribes, but it was located too far away from both the agency and the camps of his people to give any real protection. The small detachment of infantry stationed at Camp Brown could not reach his people in time to defend them against the frequent war parties of Sioux, Arapahoes, or Cheyennes. Those enemy warriors killed many white people, too. Washakie and Agent Irwin brought these facts to the attention of the Great White Father in Washington, but nothing came of their pleas for more protection.

Enemies continued to attack. Finally, in 1871, the government did move Camp Brown to the Shoshone Indian Reservation. A large number of troops were transferred and placed at Camp Brown for the protection of the Shoshone as set out in the treaty.

Enemy war parties continued to kill and destroy, but the Shoshones were both better prepared for them, and were much better protected. In 1874, after a violent attack by Arapahoes who killed both white and Shoshones, a force of U.S. Calvalry under command of Captain Bates, along with 20 enlisted Shoshone scouts, 167 Shoshone warriors led by Chief Washakie, and citizens from Camp Brown, pursued the Arapaho into the Big Horn Mountains in Wyoming territory. They found the enemy in a gorge at the base of a high bluff. All responsibility for the plan of attack was given to Chief Washakie. Captain Bates showed himself incompetent, even giving confusing orders to the warriors. During the confusion, Washakie and some of his men dashed out under enemy fire and saved the life of a white officer. The soldiers acknowledged that they had never seen such daring and bravery. The battle lasted four hours, but Washakie's competent leadership caused a complete victory over the enemy. This battle, known as the "Bates Battle," would ever afterward be strong tribute to the valor and ability of Washakie and his Shoshone warriors! It would be known as one of the famous conflicts in Wyoming's pioneer history.

In 1874, a short time after the victory, Washakie called for a great buffalo hunt. It was a tribal custom each fall to go on a buffalo hunt of several moons' duration. The hunt was held after the harvest of the food they had planted at the government's direction. On this hunt, no one was left behind except those too old to go, like Sacajawea, who was now about 90 winters old. In preparation for the hunt, there were dances and much feasting just as in former days. Chief Washakie recalled his youthful adventures and told hunting tales; he prophesied that Dama Uppa would give them plenty of game. They broke camp and went across the Owl Creek Mountains. The weather was cold and stormy. Scouts looked for the buffalo and all people were excitedly awaiting their report. When the herds were spotted, the people sang with joy. Before dawn the next day,

Washakie rode in the lead of the long column of hunters and surveyed the country through field glasses. He saw countless black specks which were the far-off grazing buffalo. The line of men spread out and awaited the command of Washakie. When he did so, the noise and commotion were terrific as the hunters bore down upon the animals. Older men shot arrows, killing the old-time way; younger men used rifles.

After it was all over, the women gathered up the meat and butchered it. No part of the animal was wasted. Even the hoofs, horns and tendons were utilized. The horns were carved into spoons and cooking utensils and dishes, the hoofs made into glue, and back tendons and sinews used by the women as sewing thread. It was so different from the way the white man hunted, for whites shot down for sport and then let nearly all of the animals rot upon the plain!

This was to be the last great hunt for the Shoshones. Cattle would now replace the buffalo as their food. They must raise grain, for bread would become a substitute for much of the meat they had always eaten.

69

Washakie fought his last battle in 1876, when the Sioux defied the whites. Chief Washakie was asked to scout for General Crook and also to counsel Crook in Indian ways of fighting. The Chief also agreed to the government's request that the Shoshones furnish at least three thousand warriors to help fight the Sioux.

Washakie did not accompany Crook's expedition against the Sioux when the General set out on the march that he called the Bighorn and Yellowstone Expedition. This Army column set out from Fort Fetterman, on May 29, 1876, and went into

Painting by Ralph Tillman

Montana. The Chief himself did not immediately go
with the soldiers because he desired to first recruit
more warriors. However, he did send a detachment
of scouts and warriors with Crook. Among the scouts
were Washakie's two sons, Dick (Coo-coosh) and
Bishop (Ga-na-yah) who was Sergeant of Shoshone
scouts.

Scouts and warriors of the Crow Tribe also
joined the Indian Auxiliary Force.

The Army traveled northward and eastward in
the direction of the Sioux enemy, and soon entered
Sioux territory. When they approached a place
where a great shaft of stone arose high above the
forest, all the Indians, marching, were filled with awe
and reverence, when they saw it. It was a sacred
place to all Indians, as well as to the Sioux. It was
called by Shoshone people, Beah Agwhy Guyhre,
Grizzly Bear's Lodge. Shoshones, and different tribes,
as well, told stories about this Rock arising above
dark trees and a winding, green-banked stream
French trappers named Belle Fourche. Indians would
go to the sacred rock to pray to the Great Spirit
Above All and seek a vision. This was a sacred place
yet no one then knew that in a distant time it would

be called by white men the irreverent name *Devil's Tower.*

As said, Crook's Indian Auxiliaries knew that they were now in Sioux territory. Ga-na-yah, with white name Bishop, quickly advised the General that his army should leave the vicinity immediately. Go around the rock, but march another way. Enemy eyes must be watching them. General Crook took heed of Ga-na-yah's wise warning, and they marched past the rock another way and out of sight of it.

On the morning of June 17, as the troops rested beside Rosebud Creek in Montana, the Sioux attacked. There was terrible fighting, lasting at least six hours. Several times the troops were nearly vanquished by the attacking Sioux and Cheyenne warriors. Had it not been for a brave counterattack by the Shoshone and Crow warriors, Crook's entire Army would have been overcome. When the fighting was over and the enemy had left, General Crook exultantly claimed the victory. The victory that day at Rosebud Creek, however, plainly belonged to the Shoshone and Crow warriors.

General Crook's Bighorn and Yellowstone Expedition against the Sioux marched away from the area of that battle. It did not join General Custer's detachment at the Bighorn River as had first been planned, only because of timely and wise advice, given once more by the Shoshone scouts, who warned that there was too great a danger in joining Custer; too many of the enemy to fight. General Crook's acceptance of this warning saved the lives of his Army. Undoubtedly, his soldiers were thereby prevented from sharing the same destruction as Yellow Hair Custer at the Bighorn.

In the opinion of white people, the Shoshone warriors, always held peaceable towards whites by their leader, except during this trouble with the Sioux, were not deserving of much credit. This disregard of the Shoshone warriors' great prowess and ability would ever afterward continue, quite unjustly, in the minds of most white people.

However, after the fighting with Sioux enemy was over, Chief Washakie would frequently gather his tribesmen about him, and they would discuss those battles. The Chief would encourage his people by proudly telling them that their warriors were the best of all fighters, better by far that even any white man soldiers. He would call his sons, Dick and Bishop and all other scouts and warriors who had taken part in Rosebud Battle to him and praise them for their excellence. He would remind them all how they had saved the lives of Crook's soldiers. Nor would he forget to also give due credit to the Crow scouts and warriors for their help.

Then, white man's government did honor the Shoshone Tribe for their part in the Rosebud Battle, when the President of the United States, Ulysses S. Grant, presented Washakie with a beautiful saddle richly decorated with silver as a symbol of the country's gratitude.

Washakie, deeply moved, stood long silent, but at last spoke. "When a favor is shown a Frenchman, he feels it in his head, and his tongue speaks," said the Chief, "but when a kindness is shown to an Indian he feels it in his heart, and the heart has no tongue. I have spoken."

In further recognition of the many ways Chief Washakie had aided the U.S. government, Fort Brown was renamed Fort Washakie in 1878.

It was indeed difficult, as time went by, for the Shoshones to concentrate on the farming prescribed by the U.S. government. Many tribesmen were discontented, and some so restless that they joined other bands of Indians, such as the Bannocks, to live again the wild and free life. It was hard for the men not to go to war or to hunt whenever they wished, as they had done in earlier days. They were like birds in cages. The older ones could not remold their lives; the young hated the restraint. Yet the government was much pleased with Washakie's efforts and treated him well. Again and again Washakie himself was to see how his sacred Medicine helped him to surpass all troubles that came his way and helped him to lighten his peoples' burdens.

In 1878, the white man's government chose to place the Arapaho Tribe on the Wind River Reservation, now home of the Shoshones. Arapahoes came in poor condition, half-starved and many sick. They had been wanderers, fighting with other tribes, as well as with white people. Many of them had sided with the Sioux and had fought Custer at the Bighorn, but now they had come to the Warm Valley asking for help, and asking to live with their old enemies the Shoshones, on their Reservation. The U.S. government wished this to be so, and sent them to share the Wind River Reservation with the Shoshones. The Shoshones said this would never do. They could not and would not accept their ancient enemies. It would only make for bad trouble. And there was trouble for both peoples from the time the Arapaho arrived.

Rev. John Roberts, good friend of Chief Washakie

Photo courtesy of the Pioneer Museum, Lander, Wyoming

Washakie, however, urged his chiefs and his people to have patience and try as much as possible to be tolerant of the Arapahoes and treat them with kindness and understanding. Gradually, then although still finding it difficult to unite socially with each other, the two tribes got along, living side by side. The government treated both tribes with fairness and equality, giving each tribe its proper rights and assistance. Washakie, from then on, would always feel that this good had come about mainly from aid given him by his Medicine as well as his own fervent desire for and belief in brotherhood for all men, even ancient enemies.

Christianity came easily to the Shoshones, in some respects, but the tradition of their fathers, their tribal tradition, could never be completely discarded. They always revered the "Great Father," Dama Uppa, to whose abode beyond the sun their spirits would sometime go, after their death. For Washakie to forget and forsake entirely his sacred Medicine and his ancient beliefs, which were his very life, was to do the impossible. He accepted the precepts of Christianity brought to his people by white missionary priests who taught Christianity and the Fatherhood of God, yet he never forbade his people their old tribal customs and religion.

The best loved and most influential to the Shoshones of the white missionary priests, was the Episcopalian minister, Reverend John Roberts, who had originally come from Wales. Coming to minister to the Shoshones in 1883, Father Roberts had great sympathy for the tribesmen, and they for him. Washakie became his very good and reliable friend.

Sometimes Washakie would sit holding his old pipe. Its engraved symbols and the silver wisp of horse hair from his favorite Bannock pony attached to its shaft, were like living things to him. He would dream of the bygone day and his deeds of honor. In his mind's eye he saw the Medicine Wheel and the teachers, old in wisdom, who had taught him the Way of Life. He saw his mother, his father, and his first wife, Crimson Dawn. He lived through the many battles he had fought and won. He felt in his hand, again, the faithful battle ax which he had always carried with him to war. Everything of importance in his life passed before his vision, while he held his pipe.

Around midsummer each year, a Sun Dance
would be held. One year the chief Medicine Man,
Basil, announced the time of the Sun Dance. The
Sun Dance always lasted three days, during which
the participants could neither eat nor drink. They
prayed to Dama Uppa as they danced, giving thanks
for His great gift to man, the sun. Most importantly,
they gave thanks for blessings bestowed upon them
by Dama Uppa. Some of the dancers would pray for
cure of a sickness. Others asked for favorable answer
to an important request. In olden times of the tribe a
dancing warrior would ask for a safe return from a
warpath, although these days warpaths were no
longer undertaken. Now though, as always in the
past, all the dancers would pray for the safety and
welfare of their families and the tribe.

The Sun Dance Ceremony took place in an
enclosure constructed of twelve cottonwood poles,
with a center pole upon which were hung twelve
eagle feathers from that sacred bird and the symbolic
head of a buffalo.

Watching the Sun Dance on the last day,
Washakie thought of all the warriors he had known
in his youth and long life. Now only Norkuk and Basil

79

were left. When the ceremony was concluded, he asked Norkuk and Basil to aid him in a council. Thus, the whole tribe gathered that night around him at the big council fire. Although quite aged now Washakie looked all the great Chieftain as he sat in the center of his leaders. He looked about him and picked out his sons and grandsons, and old friends who had grown to manhood with him. Beyond them, he saw the ring of warriors and the women and children.

After the throng of people had sung a chant of praise and tribute to Chief Washakie's leadership throughout the very many winters he had led them, he spoke to them, and his voice still carried easily to the outermost edge of the circle. He said they now lived upon the land that would belong to them for all time to come, and where they would be free. Gone were the days of war, and their lives must be forever peaceful. The opportunity was now theirs to become worthy men and women of the tribe.

Then Washakie presented to his people the Tribal Pipe of Peace. It was to be used at future Shoshone councils. It was the pipe, he explained, which the wise men of the Medicine Wheel who had taught him the Truth of Mankind had entrusted him to secure in far-off Minnesota to test his courage and fortitude. Now, he entrusted this pipe to them, to remember him by in days to come after he had gone on to the land of Dama Uppa, the Great Father Who Lives in the sun. They would smoke the Pipe as a symbol of faith and trust and confidence. It would be given into the safekeeping of Basil.

Fifteen more winters Washakie spent with his people. Often the peace pipe they called Tribal Pipe of Peace was smoked. Washakie's mind had remained sharp and his back straight in spite of his great age. His every act and thought were directed towards the good of all.

While President Chester A. Arthur visited Fort Washakie on the Wind River Reservation, he was taken all around the Reservation. When he was shown the big hot springs that were located at what is now the town of Themopolis, Wyoming, he was much impressed. Chief Washakie told him that his Shoshone people would often bathe in the waters of these springs. The tribesmen called it the "Healing Waters", for it possessed healing properties. It healed aching joints. Thereupon President Aruthur

immediately plunged into the waters and happily
soaked himself. And after this, that very evening, the
Shoshones gave the president a big celebration and
welcome, with feasting and an exhibition of tribal
dancing.

In 1895 the U.S. Indian Inspector counseled
with the leaders of the Shoshone and Arapaho
tribes, to discuss the Great Hot Springs. Still recalled
was the visit of President Arthur and his bath in the
healing waters; and by now, all the white people
wished to buy the springs for their use and to own
them. They also wished to purchase at least ten miles
of the land surrounding the springs, so it could be
settled and used by the whites. The white people
dearly wished this. However, neither the Shoshones
nor the Arapahoes wished to sell to the whites. The
Tribes said that whites were free to use those Healing
Waters, bathe in them, but no payment was desired.
And Washakie would tell his people that it was good
to allow white people to use the springs, to help
them, even though the Waters were not sold.
Washakie would say, Dama Uppa had given them to
be used by all people, to heal them. Harken, then to

this, he would say to his people, as well as to all who would listen.

Reverend John Roberts tried hard to persuade Washakie and the Arapaho Chief Sharp Nose, to sell the Healing Waters to the white people, and at last Washakie gave in to this plea of his good friend. Reverend Roberts thought the money could be used to help the tribe, and Washakie knew of tribe members in need of money. Go ahead then, said the Shoshone Chief, he would agree to take money to pay for those waters. Let the white men have that land surrounding the springs, that he wished, too, in return for some money. He accepted, even though the Arapahoes still refused.

To himself, however, sometimes he would say, wearily, that if he said "No" to the whites, they would take it all, anyway, like they took all else they desired. And yet, when he spoke to people, he would say, cheerfully, "Shoshones still have that small hot spring on the reservation near Fort Washakie Agency. It is enough."

*   *   *   *   *

On a cold February day in the year 1900, in the simple cabin which his good friend Father Roberts had helped him build, the ailing leader lay upon his narrow bed. The reservation doctor attending him had advised everyone except Washakie, himself that the chief had not much longer to live. The doctor did not realize that an Indian's strong "sixth sense" tells him things in a way that few white men understand. Washakie know he was going to die; so he said to the doctor that today he was going home. Soon he would be there. The doctor shook his head and whispered some words to Father Roberts, who sat in a chair at the bedside. The Chief signaled to his friend to come closer so he might speak to him. The minister rose and bent his ear to Washakie's weak lips.

"My good friend," Washakie began, and his voice seemed to gain power as he spoke, "which is the best for me to follow, now—the white man's Christ which you have caused me to follow, or the sacred beliefs of my own people that I have always known? Which will take me along the Path to the Great Father? Please tell Washakie, does the Indian receive his just due in your heaven, or is your heaven meant only for the white man? Even though I have taken your Christ to my heart, will He take me now?

Will Washakie's own Great Father help him? Washakie must know these things. His heart is troubled by these matters which he must know before his spirit shall leave him forever."

Reverend Roberts' white-bearded, kindly face broke into a reassuring smile. "My dear old friend, be at once and always comforted," he said. "The white man's God and your Great Father, Dama Uppa, are one and the same. To God, there is no difference in the color of a man's skin. In heaven, we are all one."

The old Chieftain breathed a thankful sign and closed his eyes and rested. A few moments later he opened his eyes again and saw the minister and the doctor standing close to him.

"You two, still here?" he whispered, his strength now beginning to fail him. "Only you? Washakie must see. . . family, friends, my leaders. . ."

"Hush," the doctor cautioned, soothingly, "save yourself, Sir, and rest."

"No," Washakie repeated, in his manner a faint flicker of the former majestic authority, "Norkuk, my leaders. . . my family. Send them here to me!"

Word was sent out and immediately the people he asked for arrived and gathered about his bedside.

"Washakie has ever trod the Path," said the Chief, pulling himself up a little and looking at them all. "Washakie has trod the Path for his Tribe and for all men. Footsteps of Washakie. . .have led. . .ever upward along the Path of Brotherhood."

Here Washakie's breath became weaker. They all bent low over him to catch the next words: "Keep trust . . .with the white men and your Shoshone brothers, and they will never fail you. Follow. . .in my footsteps! I hope that what I have said will enter your ears and your hearts."

Chief Washakie's funeral.
His grave is located at Fort Washakie, Wyoming in the Chief Washakie Cemetery.

Courtesy of the Pioneer Museum, Lander, Wyoming

The chief withdrew his right hand which he had kept under the bed covers. In his hand was the crucifix Father Roberts had once given him. He looked at it and his lips moved silently as he said the Lord's Prayer in the Shoshone language. Then, he placed his left hand over his talisman, which for more than a hundred winters he had worn about his neck. The sacred symbol upon the flat stone disk glowed.

* * * * *

Chief Washakie was given a full military funeral. He lies buried in a cemetery on his reservation in his warm valley of the Wind River which he loved so well. Never since, and never before, has an Indian burial been so honored by white and red men alike. For never was there an Indian more revered for fighting his battles so successfully and then giving his life so fully to peace, good will and brotherhood, than was Washakie of the Shoshones.

My name is Washakie, the Rattler!
It is good,
My life will be good.

Further Readings

Ellison, R. S. *Fort Bridger, A Brief History*. Casper, WY: Historical Landmark Commission of Wyoming, 1931.

Hebard, Grace Raymond. *Washakie: An Account of Indian Resistance of the Covered Wagon and Union Pacific Railroad Invasions of the Territory.* Reprint. New York: AMS Press, 1982.

_____. *Washakie: Chief of the Shoshones.* Reprint. Lincoln: University of Nebraska Press, 1996.

The Glorious Quest of Chief Washakie